# Then and Now

# Travel

## Vicki Yates

**Heinemann**
**LIBRARY**

Chicago, Illinois

Customer Service 888-454-2279
Visit our website at www.heinemannraintree.com

Designed by Victoria Bevan and Joanna Hinton-Malivoire
Photo research by Ruth Smith and Q2A Solutions
Printed and bound in China by South China Printing Co. Ltd.

12 11 10 09 08
10 9 8 7 6 5 4 3 2 1

ISBN-10: 1-4034-9831-8 (hc)    1-4034-9839-3 (pb)

**The Library of Congress has cataloged the first edition of this book as follows:**

Yates, Vicki.
   Travel / Vicki Yates.
      p. cm. -- (Then and now)
   Includes bibliographical references and index.
   ISBN-13: 978-1-4034-9831-1 (hc)
   ISBN-13: 978-1-4034-9839-7 (pb)
   1. Travel--History--Juvenile literature. I. Title.
   G175.Y38 2008
   910--dc22                                            2007014729
                              2553

**Acknowledgements**
The publishers would like to thank the following for permission to reproduce photographs: Alamy pp. **4** (Frances Roberts/Alamy),
**22** (Bill Boston); Airbus pp. **5**, **17**; AP Images p. **18**; Courtesy of The Bancroft Library p. **20** (University of California, Berkeley);
Bionik Media p. **6**; Daimler Chrysler p. **9**; Ford Media pp. **5**, **11**; Honda p. **23**; NASA pp. **19**, **23**; Phil Derner, Jr p. **7** (Airliners.
net); Photolibrary.com pp. **13** (David Messent), **14** (Index Stock Imagery), **15** (Photo Researchers, Inc), **16** (Science Photo
Library), **21** (Index Stock Imagery); Puget Sound Maritime Historical Society pp. **12**, **23**; San Francisco Public Library p. **8**;
Science & Society Picture Library p. **10** (Science Museum Archive); Shutterstock p. **5**.

Cover photograph of plane reproduced with permission of Alamy (BL Images Ltd) and photograph of horse and cart reproduced
with permission of Getty Images (Robert Harding).
Back cover photograph reproduced with permission of Photolibrary.com/Index Stock Imagery.

Every effort has been made to contact copyright holders of any material reproduced in this book. Any omissions will be
rectified in subsequent printings if notice is given to the publishers.

# Contents

# What Is Travel?

Traveling is moving from place to place.

People can travel in many ways.

Long ago it took a long time to travel.

Today it takes a short time
to travel.

Long ago animals helped people travel.

Today buses help people travel.

# Travel by Road

Long ago cars were slow.

Today cars can be fast.

# Travel by Water

Long ago boats used sails to move.

Today boats can use engines
to move.

# Travel by Rail

Long ago trains were slow.

Today trains can be fast.

# Travel in the Sky

Long ago planes were small.

Today planes can be big.

Long ago it was hard to travel far.

Today we can travel into space.

# Let's Compare

Long ago travel was very different.

How is travel different today?

# What Is It?

tool

Long ago this tool was used for travel.
Do you know what it is?

Answer on p. 24

# Picture Glossary

**engine**  a machine that makes things work

**sail**  a piece of cloth attached to a boat. It fills with air to help the boat move.

**space**  the area outside Earth where the stars and planets are found

# Index

**Answer to question on p. 22**: It is a starting handle. People used it to start the engine in cars and other vehicles.

**Note to Parents and Teachers**

**Before reading**: Ask children how they get to school. Have they ever been on a train or a plane? Did it go fast or slow?

**After reading**: Using catalogs or magazines, ask children to cut out pictures of different vehicles. Make a collage of all the different ways people travel today. Ask children how travel has changed. Write captions under the different vehicles that say how they have changed over time, such as their shape, speed, and accessiblity to the public.

You can support children's nonfiction literacy skills by helping them use the table of contents, headings, picture glossary, and index.